Copyright

MW00364968

About the Authors

NoR is the collective writing name of a group of researchers.

They believe that the true purpose of education is to stimulate people to think for themselves. Their intention is for their writing to inspire people to look beneath the often misleading 'veneer' on information that is promulgated by many official sources.

The authors can be contacted through their website at www.thenatureofreality.com

CONTENTS

Introduction

Module 1   Your Limited Perception of Reality

The world that seems so solid and separate from you can be shown by quantum physics to be a trick of the senses. The apparent 'materiality' of the world is no more 'real' than a dream image.
Incredible as these statements may sound, this first module takes you step by step along a path that explores and explains many astounding concepts, such as:
Is there such a thing as a solid object?
What is a 'thought' made of?
Is there actually an 'out there' out there?

Module 1 Test Yourself Questions

Module 2   How Beliefs Affect Your Life

Generally, people think that the word consciousness refers to something that is a by-product of the brain. Therefore, you may be surprised to learn that science has been unable to provide any convincing evidence to support this widely held belief.
There are some beliefs about life which are so ingrained that you may think they are facts about life. This can cause many problems. Understanding how beliefs affect your life will enable you to change those beliefs that adversely affect you for more beneficial ones.
In this module you learn more about the true nature of consciousness and the creative power of 'thought'. The 'placebo effect', as used by the medical profession, provides evidence that beliefs have far-reaching implications that you may not have previously considered.

Module 2 Test Yourself Questions

Module 3   The True Nature of Time

Classical science taught that 'time' was a constant throughout the universe. Einstein proved that 'time' is relative and therefore not a constant.
Although experience seems to indicate that 'time' started somewhere in the distant 'past' and continues relentlessly through the 'present' and into the 'future', this experience can be shown by quantum physics to be illusory. It can be shown that past, present and future exist simultaneously; incredible as this may sound, it means you can learn to manipulate 'time'.
This module explains how to make practical use of this new understanding of 'time'.

Module 3 Test Yourself Questions

Module 4   Insights Into Reincarnation & Death

All religious traditions are founded on the existence of two separate realms, the 'spiritual' and the 'physical', and the inevitability of 'death'. In addition, eastern traditions teach about reincarnation and the law of Karma, which are dependent on a sequential progression of time.
Quantum physics has forced a complete re-think on the concepts of 'time' and the existence of a solid and separate world.
Extrapolating the concepts from the previous 3 modules shows you that the 'classical' view of 'physical' and 'spiritual' can no longer be supported. However, the 'new' view is much more exciting and liberating, particularly with regard to 'death'.

Module 4 Test Yourself Questions

Module 5   The Source of All 'Being'

Many people 'feel' that there is more to life than just producing the next generation of humanity and trying to do the best they can in their lifetime. The difficulty has been to provide 'scientific evidence' for something that exists beyond time and space.

Physicist Alain Aspect and his colleagues were able to confirm a 'transcendent reality' beyond the apparent 'material reality' of space-time. Could this be the source of our true nature and have provided the concept of 'God' found in all spiritual traditions?

This module explores the mysterious nature of this 'transcendent reality' which is the source of all 'personal' experiences.

Module 5 Test Yourself Questions

Module 6   The Nature of Illness & How to Stay Well

Dr. Albert Schweitzer said "Each patient carries his own doctor inside him."

The 'placebo effect' is a medically proven phenomenon. Using the findings of the medical profession in conjunction with the findings of quantum physics, you will learn how 'thoughts' play a crucial role in why people become ill.

This module presents a radically new understanding of your 'body' that will impact on all areas of your 'health'. Once you understand how you become 'ill', you will be able to adopt a new and natural approach to staying 'well'.

Module 6 Test Yourself Questions

Module 7   The True Nature of Dreams

The philosopher Lao Tzu fell asleep and dreamt he was a butterfly. Upon wakening he asked, "Am I a man who has just been dreaming he was a butterfly? Or a sleeping butterfly now dreaming he is a man?"
New insights into consciousness show that this quote is not as fanciful as it might appear.
It is unfortunate that many people associate the word 'dream' with the word 'unreal', because this way of thinking sets up barriers to understanding states of consciousness.
This module explores the 'dream state of consciousness' in further detail using visual analogies that you can easily relate to. It shows how an understanding of the 'dream state of consciousness' can be used in a practical way.

Module 7 Test Yourself Questions

Module 8   The True Nature of World Events

Physicist John Wheeler said: "Useful as it is under everyday circumstances to say that the world exists 'out there' independent of us, that view can no longer be upheld."
If there is not a world existing 'out there independent of us', then it begs the question; what is a world event such as an earthquake involving thousands of people?
The consequences of John Wheeler's statement require you to reassess everything you think you know about yourself and your world and therefore what you think of as 'world events' and 'other people'.
This module explores those consequences and provides you with explanations that are unprecedented and astounding, but nonetheless supported by sound scientific discoveries and the most ancient wisdom philosophies.

Module 8 Test Yourself Questions

Module 9   The Magical Approach to Living

You may be accustomed to thinking of yourself as just flesh and blood; that you only have logic and intellect to navigate your way through the challenges of life.
Nothing could be further from the truth.
This is a very exciting time as science reaches conclusions that support many of the concepts put forward in the ancient wisdom philosophies.
Physicist Professor Amit Goswami has stated quite clearly that "matter, energy and consciousness are the same thing"; that "everything, including matter, exists in and is manipulated from consciousness".
These statements revolutionize the old ways of thinking and herald in a new world view.
But this new world view can only be brought into effect through a better understanding of the nature of reality.
This final module brings together all the concepts explored and explained in the previous modules. It offers a radically new understanding of reality and a new and seemingly 'magical' approach to living in which you will no longer feel a victim of circumstances, because you will know how to actively initiate your own experiences.

Module 9 Test Yourself Questions

Introduction

The world view presented by so-called mainstream sources has left many people dissatisfied, and with good reason.

Most religions teach that we live in a universe presided over by a loving, peaceful and all-powerful God, but fail to explain why immense human suffering can be seen or experienced in life, particularly in 'natural' disasters such as a tsunami or earthquake.

Classical science, with its mechanical view of the universe, has failed to explain phenomena such as telepathy, remote viewing or out of body experiences, to name just a few. These phenomena are far too well documented to be dismissed, so they must be incorporated into a plausible world view.

'New age' belief systems borrow from the eastern philosophies and talk about the 'wholeness' of reality or that everything is 'one', but then continue to philosophise about the nature of reality in the 'dualistic' terms of 'spiritual' and 'physical'. These belief systems are further confused by the consideration of 3 separate states, namely, mind, body, spirit.

A number of eminent physics professors have stated quite clearly that matter, energy and consciousness are the same thing, which would indicate that there cannot be these normally accepted 3 separate states of mind, body and spirit.

Although the progress of quantum physics has brought science closer towards what the ancient eastern philosophies have been alluding to for thousands of years, neither quantum physics nor eastern philosophy explains those ideas in words and concepts that are of practical use in everyday life.

It may therefore seem impossible to find a way through the world's minefield of beliefs and dogmas without wasting years studying systems which turn out to be unsatisfactory or even worthless; which fail to answer any of the big questions about life and world events.

It is obvious that there is something missing in the prevailing world view presented by the mainstream sources.

Einstein once said, "A problem cannot be solved using the same thoughts or approach which caused it in the first place".

This book provides a radically new approach.

Although the concepts are both astounding and challenging, they are supported by discoveries at the cutting edge of quantum physics.

The staggering implications of this new approach will completely change your view of who you think you are and what life really is.

Module 1

Your Limited Perception of Reality

Sooner or later, in one form or another, everyone will ask themselves these questions:

Who am I?

Is there a purpose to life?

What happens to me when I die?

To gain some insights into the answers to these questions requires a good understanding of the nature of reality.

But as you will see, the nature of reality is far stranger than you can imagine.

Discoveries at the cutting edge of quantum physics about the true nature of reality give radical, new and exciting insights into topics that you may have considered the realm of metaphysics rather than the realm of science.

The consequences of these discoveries will lead you to a completely different view of your actions and the actions of other people; of what you think is possible and what is not possible.

To start the exploration of the true nature of reality you first need to consider this question:

How do you experience reality?

But more specifically, how do you experience your personal reality?

This is a subject often taken for granted, but well worth pondering for a moment or two.

It's generally accepted that day to day experiences are received through the five senses, which are touch, taste, sight, hearing and smell.

But do you think your senses tell you everything about your day to day reality?

To help understand this point requires an examination of some of the senses in more detail.

Starting with the sense of sight, consider what science says about the light spectrum.

Most people will have encountered, in school science lessons, an experiment where a beam of white light was shone through a prism to see what happened.

The white beam was refracted by the prism into a band showing seven colours starting with red, followed by orange, yellow, green, blue, indigo and violet.

A natural effect of this is seen in a rainbow, which is produced by the refraction of light by raindrops.

This effect is very interesting because, although you see this spectrum of colours, science says that it is part of the electromagnetic spectrum, which contains other frequencies in addition to visible light.

In fact, visible light makes up only a very small part of the electromagnetic spectrum.

Although science shows that other frequencies exist beyond the visible light spectrum, your eyes do not see them.

So, using the information from your sense of sight, you might be tempted to think that there are no such things as ultra-violet, infra-red, x-rays, gamma rays, radio waves and microwaves.

A similar experience occurs when another of the senses, namely hearing, is considered.

The human ear has been shown to perceive a range of sounds in the region of 15 Hertz to 20,000 Hertz (the more an object vibrates, the higher the frequency, which is measured in Hertz).

Generally for humans, frequencies beyond this range are not audible and therefore do not appear to exist.

But science demonstrates that for certain animals other frequencies are audible and are part of their everyday life.

In fact, many creatures have hearing ranges that quite significantly exceed the human range, for example bats and dolphins as well as cats and dogs.

These examples show that your senses do not tell you the whole story, but what is most interesting is that your senses actually 'filter out' more than they 'let through'.

This interesting topic can be taken one step further into what may seem a more bizarre area to those not familiar with the 'quantum' world.

It is not necessary to explain any of the complex maths of quantum physics, but it is necessary to explain some 'basic science' to understand the impact this subject has on your everyday reality.

To give you an idea of how exciting the science part of this is, consider the following question:

Is there such a thing as a solid object?

A ridiculous question you might think, but is it?

To gain a clearer understanding of what things are made of requires a closer look.

The floor you stand on for instance.

It feels pretty solid doesn't it?

But what is it really made of?

Wood?

Brick?

Concrete?

That is certainly its appearance, but what is being referred to here requires an explanation from science as to what things are really made of.

Scientists have always wanted to know how the world works in order to be able to understand the mystery of 'life'.

They thought that by knowing how everything worked they would be able to predict what would happen next; they were on a search for the 'theory of everything'.

Basic science says that everything is made of atoms, which at one time was thought to be the smallest piece of matter.

Having discovered the atom, scientists then proceeded to try and find out what that was made of.

They discovered that atoms have a nucleus surrounded by a number of orbiting electrons, which revolve about the nucleus at fantastic speeds.

As well as moving parts, they also discovered that there are spaces between each atom and its neighbour.

The scientists continued their quest to find the smallest piece of matter and soon realised that the nucleus of an atom is made of even smaller pieces, which they called neutrons and protons.

They have since found even smaller 'pieces of matter' and given them names like quarks, neutrinos and even more recently strings.

But surely they have to be made of something too?

Now this is where it becomes slightly embarrassing for the scientists.

The closer they have tried to look at all these 'pieces of matter' the less they can determine what they are actually made of.

'Matter' seems to disappear before their eyes.

So, at the cutting edge of quantum physics, the best that can be determined is that 'matter' is made of 'energy'; but no-one is quite sure what 'energy' is.

With this explanation, now reconsider the question previously asked:

Is there such a thing as a solid object?

The floor, which seems so solid to your sense of touch, is actually composed of lots of tiny atoms.

These atoms are far from stationary.

They have parts that move about at high speed.

And there are spaces between the atoms.

Each one of these atoms is made of even smaller' bits' which are made of, well, 'energy', but scientists are not really sure what that is.

Now you know why the question is not so ridiculous after all, just think about it again:

Is there such a thing as a solid object?

You have to admit that your sense of touch says yes, but what science has discovered about the nature of a so-called solid object might make you re-think that answer.

Contemplation of this topic has led physicist Harold Puthoff to reassess Albert Einstein's famous equation, $E=mc^2$.

Puthoff states that Einstein's equation should be thought of as a recipe for how much energy is required to give the appearance of matter, that is, the appearance of something 'solid'.

Now that you have had a chance to see how your senses can fool you, here is another mind-boggling question!

Do you think it is possible to know the true nature of reality just using the five senses you have?

If you consider the information covered so far, it is fair to say quite unequivocally that you are unable to rely on your senses to tell you about the true nature of the world you inhabit.

You have to admit that, at best, your five senses only provide a version of the true nature of reality.

This point becomes clearer if you regard the five senses as a set of 'filters'.

In the case of your everyday reality, these filters actually filter out more than they let through, as shown with the simple examples of light and sound frequencies.

You may be wondering:

Why do we have this filtering system?

To help with the answer, consider this question:

What do you think would happen if suddenly your eyes could see light waves in the ultra-violet and infra-red ranges and your ears could sense ultra-sonic and sub-sonic sound?

Think about it!

Consider for a moment what it would be like to suddenly be aware of all that information!

It is reasonable to say that you would experience a totally different world from the one you experience now, a totally different reality.

Having considered some of your senses; how they 'work' and the reason for it, this topic can be expanded, but with a change of approach.

Consider the world you construct in a dream, the people, the buildings, the landscape etc.

Where do they exist?

In your head?

In your mind?

In your imagination?

Would you describe yourself as 'conscious' when you are dreaming?

You can probably accept that you are experiencing a level of consciousness whilst dreaming, otherwise you would be 'unconscious' in which case you would not be aware of anything.

Therefore, it seems reasonable to describe your dream life as a 'state of consciousness'.

You now need to consider what is happening when you are in the dream 'state of consciousness'.

In your dreams you can experience all the activities of your everyday reality, such as walking, talking, meeting people, driving a car.

You can see mountains, rivers, fields, houses, towns, cities, cars, people etc.

When you move in your dream-world, the dream floor you walk on seems solid enough.

In fact, all the objects and people you encounter in your dream state appear solid and external to you and you interact with them accordingly.

This is an extremely important point, because while you are deeply enmeshed in your dream it is your total reality and you are aware of no other.

It is only when you wake up that you realise that all the objects and people that seemed solid and external to you, were not.

They were all creations within consciousness produced by you.

Whilst you are deep within that state of consciousness called dream, everything is completely real to you as the dreamer, as anyone who has had a frightening dream will know.

It is only when you awake from your dream that you consider the dream experiences and images to be 'unreal'.

So far so good, but now it's time to ask another seemingly crazy question.

What are the objects in a dream made of?

As this question is explored its relevance will become apparent.

It would seem reasonable to start with the statement:

Everything has to be made of something.

But does that include even a thought?

To help understand this a little better, consider the research that has been carried out into what happens when people dream.

There have been many laboratory experiments using an electroencephalograph to record brain activity during the state of dream.

The graphs produced from the experiments have demonstrated that 'energy' is emitted by the brain. (Energy! It's that word again).

Of particular interest is the fact that a graph of the brain activity of an alert, awake person is very similar to a graph of a person in dreaming sleep.

But what is being recorded on these graphs of brain activity; are they actually recording the energy of a thought?

To develop an understanding of the 'energy of thought', consider the phenomena of telepathy and remote viewing.

What sort of energy is being used by people engaged in these phenomena?

Whatever you might think about them, telepathy and remote viewing are too well documented to deny that something very real is happening.

In case you are not familiar with the term remote viewing; it is the ability of a trained person to be situated in one location while able to 'view' another location, anywhere in the world.

This is done purely with the mind, and in many cases very detailed information about the 'remote' location has been reported.

It may sound surprising, but this very ability has been taken so seriously by both the Russian and American Secret Services, that they have used it to successfully spy on one another since the early 1970's.

Telepathy has also been taken seriously by prominent scientists as the following account will show.

Apollo 14 astronaut Edgar Mitchell, an astrophysicist as well as an astronaut, had been conducting experiments into telepathy prior to the Apollo mission.

So he decided to conduct his own, unofficial experiment whilst on the Apollo mission.

He wanted to see if the 250,000 miles between him and Earth would have any effect on telepathic communication.

The experiments were designed to see if telepathic communication could occur by transmitting various symbols on a set of cards to colleagues back on Earth.

On his return to Earth, it was discovered that the success rate of the experiment exceeded the mathematical probability of the results being due to chance alone.

These examples quite clearly show that not only is reality very different from how it appears to be, but there is energy of some sort being used in quite extraordinary ways.

They also demonstrate the use of energy in connection with 'thought', whether it is 'thought' in the waking state, the dream state or even telepathy.

So it is quite fair to say that 'thought' must be some sort of energy.

Interestingly, that is exactly what so-called solid objects are made of!

Earlier in the module it was shown that your dream state can be called 'a state of consciousness'.

In this state of consciousness you create people, places and objects and then interact with them as if they were solid, external to you and independent of you.

It was also shown that your thoughts and so-called solid objects are all energy and that any use of consciousness is also a use of energy.

It is amazing that no matter what is examined, whether 'thought' or 'solid objects', it is all comprised of this mysterious substance called energy; but no one seems to know exactly what that is.

The next step is momentous.

You now need to understand that your waking state is a state of consciousness.

At first hearing, this statement may sound implausible.

But think about it for a moment.

Is there any reason why your waking state could not be another state of consciousness similar to the dream state of consciousness?

If you construct and manipulate dream objects, which are energy, is it possible that you construct and manipulate everyday so-called solid objects, which are also energy?

The following statements by some eminent quantum physicists about the nature of reality will help you understand this concept, which is expanded upon throughout the book.

Physicist Professor Amit Goswami has stated quite clearly that

"Matter, energy and consciousness are the same thing."

Physicist Roger S Jones states:

"I had come to suspect, and now felt compelled to acknowledge, that science and the physical world were products of human imagining; that we were not the cool observers of that world, but its passionate creators. We were all poets and the world was our metaphor."

Physicist John Wheeler states:

"Useful as it is under everyday circumstances to say that the world exists 'out there' independent of us, that view can no longer be upheld."

The consequences of this module are so far-reaching that they require you to reassess everything you think you know about yourself and your world.

Module 1

Your Limited Perception of Reality

Test Yourself Questions

1.1 What does modern physics have to say about the light and sound spectrum?

1.2 How would you describe what an object is made of?

1.3 Where do dreams exist?

1.4 What are dream objects made of?

1.5 How would you describe energy?

1.6 What do energy, consciousness and matter have in common?

Module 2

How Beliefs Affect Your Life

The previous module can perhaps best be summarised in the words of the physicist Professor Amit Goswami in stating:

"Matter, energy and consciousness are the same thing."

Professor Goswami goes on further to say:

"Everything, including matter, exists in and is manipulated from consciousness. This does not mean that matter is unreal but that the reality of matter is secondary to that of consciousness, which itself is the ground of all being, including matter."

To help further understand consciousness as the ground of all being, which includes what is thought of as 'personal consciousness', consider the following analogy.

Imagine consciousness, which is the ground of all being, as an ocean.

An ocean is made up of molecules of water, each of which has its own individuality but at the same time is an integral part of the whole body of water.

In the same way, 'personal consciousness' has its own individuality but at the same time is an integral part of the whole ocean of consciousness.

To help define 'personal consciousness' a little further, consider the 'dream state'.

When you are in the 'state of consciousness' called dreaming, you still retain your sense of identity.

In other words you still feel like 'you'.

You even have a sense of body image, which you identify as being 'you'.

Therefore, you interact with anything that you do not consider as 'you' as if it is separate from and independent of 'you'.

In the dream state of consciousness you make this differentiation between 'you' and 'not you', even though this cannot be the case because all images in your dream are part of your personal state of consciousness and therefore must be part of 'you'.

Understanding this last point is extremely important because you also form all images in your waking state of consciousness using the same beliefs about what is 'you' and 'not you'.

This is, perhaps, a difficult concept to completely grasp at this stage, but it will become clearer as you progress through the book.

Ponder for a moment what was explored in Module 1 concerning the dream state of consciousness.

It was clearly shown that 'thought' is 'energy' and is extremely powerful and creative.

Whilst in your dream state of consciousness you create a whole reality of seemingly separate objects and individuals and then interact with them.

The reality you create is so convincing that whilst you are focused in it you are unaware that it is being created by 'you'.

It is so convincing that you can even create and experience emotions such as fear, anger or happiness.

To develop this concept of 'the creative power of thought' requires a consideration of the term 'a belief'.

The dictionary defines a belief as something you accept to be true.

However, just because you accept something to be true, it does not mean that it is actually true.

In other words, in the light of further information, you may need to revise your 'beliefs'.

Here are some examples of 'beliefs' that you may have changed in the light of further information:

Most people, as children, used to believe in Father Christmas, but stopped believing in him when they were told that he did not really exist.

Again, many people were taught, and probably still hold the belief today, that Christopher Columbus discovered America.

But, in actual fact, what he discovered was the West Indies.

He was trying to find a western passage to India, which is what he thought he had found, and that is why those islands are called the West Indies even to this day.

The person who was credited by the cartographer Martin Waldseemuller with the discovery of America is Amerigo Vespucci.

Some sources suggest that it is from his name that the name America is derived.

In the light of this information some people may have just changed a belief that they have held for years.

Some beliefs, like the last one perhaps, are easier to change than others.

However, some beliefs about life are so ingrained that people think they are facts about life, rather than just beliefs about life.

This is a very important point to bear in mind.

It is therefore very useful to make a list of your beliefs.

Regularly reviewing your list will show you how your beliefs are changing and which items on your list are actual facts and which ones are just beliefs.

If you are having a little trouble starting your list, then consider if you hold the following belief.

You may believe that:

As you get older it is inevitable that you become frailer and weaker.

Remember that a belief is something you accept to be true, but information gained later may show it not to be true after all.

Here is another question about beliefs you may hold.

Would you agree that:

People generally feel they are victims of circumstance; that life 'happens' to them, mostly outside of their control?

But, what if 'being a victim' is based only on a set of beliefs?

You may find this quite a challenging statement.

However, remember what has been stated about a belief being something you accept to be true, but may not be.

You may believe that you live in a world of facts.

Therefore, it may be difficult to accept that your knowledge is largely a collection of beliefs about life rather than a collection of facts about life.

Feeling that they are facts about life is what causes the most problems.

Once you realise you are dealing with beliefs, rather than unchangeable facts, then your intellect can accept that it is possible to change them.

If you wish to change a particular circumstance in your life you first have to be very sure whether you are dealing with a fact about life, or just believe it is a fact about life.

Once you are sure of this, you also need to understand that there is a difference between a desire and an expectation.

A desire is best described as something you hope will happen, but have no certainty that it will.

An expectation, however, is having complete certainty that what you want to happen will happen.

Desire can be transformed into definite expectation, but desire on its own is not enough to bring about the required change in your personal experiences.

It is easy to confuse 'a desire' with 'an expectation' and therefore become disappointed when you do not appear to get the outcome you want.

The procedure for changing beliefs, and therefore your experiences, has to start from a fundamental understanding of the difference between a fact and a belief; and between a desire and a definite expectation.

The methods for changing beliefs may be different for each person and can vary from using such techniques as visualisation to writing lists.

It is best to use whatever technique feels right for you and to remember that only a full expectation of the required change will make it happen.

With this understanding you can start to accept new beneficial beliefs in place of old limiting beliefs.

You can then conduct your daily life in the secure knowledge that your experiences will fall in line with your new beliefs about what is possible.

Consider again the belief in being a 'victim'.

Feeling like a victim of some sort can take many forms and is usually built on a collection of personal beliefs, but there are a couple of fundamental beliefs that will always be present.

They are the beliefs that it is possible to be a victim in the first place, and that there is a world that is solid, separate and external to you and therefore outside of your control.

As you become more confident in the knowledge that you only experience what you believe is possible, then you will experience fewer instances where you cast yourself in the role of 'victim'.

You should be gentle with yourself as you build your confidence in consciously initiating the experiences you want.

You may wish to start by changing what you consider to be some small aspect of your personal experiences.

As you see the required changes come about, it will give you the confidence to tackle what you consider to be more difficult challenges.

When setting your 'goals', it is important not to limit yourself by insisting on too much detail as to how and when you will create that experience for yourself.

To help with this, it is advisable to 'focus on the goal and not the obstacles' and keep in mind the difference between a desire and an expectation.

A core belief of 'expect the best' will ensure that whatever happens, it will be the best, even if intellect cannot see a logical way forward.

To further understand the power of belief, consider the use of placebo pills and placebo surgery by the medical profession.

A placebo pill is just a sugar pill with no real medication properties.

It is administered to the patient as if it is a specific drug with precise medical value which is expected by the patient to have the desired effect.

The patient believes in the doctor and believes in the treatment.

The effectiveness of these sugar pills is quite remarkable.

They have been used to treat all kinds of illness, including cancer.

Even more astounding is the result of a major trial in the USA on the placebo effect of surgery for arthritis of the knee.

A team of surgeons in Texas tested the procedure by performing the surgery on 180 patients with osteoarthritis in the knee.

Two-thirds had two different types of the surgery.

But for the remaining third of the patients, the surgeons went through the motions by giving a tranquilizer, making three incisions and pretending to do the surgery.

All participants in the study had to sign their chart to show that they understood they might receive the placebo surgery, which would not help their arthritic knee.

Most arthroscopic surgery on the knee is done to repair injured ligaments and cartilage, which doctors say is useful.

The experiment was designed to see whether the surgery helped reduce pain and increase mobility in patients with an arthritic knee.

The researchers found patients who underwent the placebo surgery were just as likely to report pain relief as those who received the real procedure.

It seems that for osteoarthritis patients, the relief is all in their heads.

Dr. Bruce Moseley, an orthopaedics professor at Baylor College in Houston and one of the study's co-authors, said

"I don't believe that arthroscopic surgery for osteoarthritis of the knee is any more beneficial than a placebo effect, and I don't recommend it."

Further evidence was shown on a television programme in the UK made for the BBC's Open University.

The researchers found that the effectiveness of all medicine, orthodox and alternative, is certainly partly due to the 'placebo effect', meaning that if you believe something will do you good then it most probably will.

The programme continued by saying that the placebo effect could demonstrate the power of a person's mind and body to heal itself, thus further illustrating how the importance of expecting a positive outcome plays an important role in the effectiveness of both alternative and orthodox medicine.

To expand the placebo effect to the area of diets, consider the statement that 'if diets really worked, there would only need to be one diet and it would work for everyone.'

As stated by Prof. Fletcher, Dr. Pine and Dr. Penman

"Diets are so ineffective in controlling weight that around 95% of people who go on one end up just as fat a year later (and sometimes fatter too)."

In a 20 year study of behavioural flexibility in British Universities and for the UK's Medical Research Council, Professor Ben Fletcher, Dr Karen Pine and Dr Danny Penman discovered that the more flexible your behaviour, the more weight you will lose.

What is really amazing about this study is that weight loss or gain had nothing to do with food consumption.

This is a powerful example demonstrating that 'what goes on in your mind determines your physical experiences'.

As further examples of how your health is affected by 'what you think', consider the following medical research findings.

Steven Greer and his colleagues of Kings College Hospital medical school in London conducted a study on breast cancer.

They found that patients with 'fighting spirit' or 'denial' were more likely to be alive and relapse-free five years after diagnosis than patients who resigned themselves to the disease.

Further to this, in a study by Brenda Penninx and her colleagues on the relationship between depression and cancer, it was found that chronically depressed non-smokers were more likely to develop cancer than smokers.

In addition, a great deal of study has been carried out on how 'natural killer cells' in the body's immune system are affected by stressful periods in a person's life.

It was clearly demonstrated that the effectiveness of the 'natural killer cells' was reduced during periods of high stress.

These findings are supported by an experiment conducted on a group of dental students.

Small holes were made in the roof of the mouths of a group of students, once during a holiday period and once just before their exams.

The wounds took on average 40% longer to heal around exam time than they did in the more relaxed holiday period.

Not only do your beliefs affect your health, they also affect how long you live.

Daniel E Moerman, PhD and Wayne B Jonas MD were able to show that non-white Chinese Americans die much earlier than would normally be expected if, according to Chinese traditions, it was indicated that they had an ill fated combination of birth date and disease.

They demonstrated that the more a person believed in the traditional Chinese culture, the more pronounced the effect.

The differences in life span, up to 6% or 7%, were not due to having Chinese genes but to having Chinese beliefs.

This powerful example shows the dire consequences of erroneous and often hidden thought patterns.

The placebo effect shows that there is more to human health and wellbeing than is currently explained by either orthodox or alternative medicine.

The conclusion that can be drawn from these examples is that the patients' powerful beliefs were the only factor at play in bringing about very real medical changes.

There are many such examples in medical journals from around the World.

The power of belief is so well recognised by the medical profession that the prescription of placebos continues on a daily basis by many doctors.

The use of placebos is a very practical example of the power of your beliefs.

Understanding the power of your beliefs is crucial to understanding how you initiate your personal experiences.

Your everyday reality is a state of consciousness in which all your experiences are based on your beliefs about what is possible and what is not possible.

This concept will continue to become clearer throughout the book and provide you with the ability to gain more creative control over every aspect of your life.

Module 2

How Beliefs Affect Your Life

Test Yourself Questions

2.1   How do you think a 'thought' is transmitted
       between people during telepathy and why does
       distance seem to have no effect on it?

2.2   How does the creative power of thought work?

2.3   How would you define what a belief is?

2.4   How would you define the difference between a
       belief and a fact?

2.5   How do placebo pills and placebo surgery work?

Module 3

The True Nature of Time

How is 'time' comprehended?

Is it just with the aid of a wristwatch, office clock or the calendar hung on the wall?

Or is it something more fundamental than these?

Is it the cycle of the Sun as it causes the shift from day to night and back again?

Certainly all of these things contribute to an awareness of time passing and a method of measuring time, but the most constant reminder of time passing is probably the least obvious.

It is the passing of your thoughts.

Your thoughts appear to follow one another in a constant stream, and so give you an impression of time passing.

But are your impressions of time correct?

You may think of time as a constant, which started at the 'Big Bang' and progressed relentlessly up to the present moment.

But time does not really exist in that way at all; what you think of as past, present and future actually exist simultaneously.

This may sound unbelievable because it seems to contradict all the experiences of your daily life.

However, as already shown, the way you experience your reality through the five senses is not how reality actually is.

Consider the following quotations from 2 eminent physicists:

Professor Brian Greene states:

"The laws of physics treat what we call past and future on a completely equal footing. Even though experience reveals over and over again that there is an arrow of how events unfold in time, this arrow seems not to be found in the fundamental laws of physics."

Albert Einstein said:

"People like us who believe in physics know that the distinction between past, present and future is only a stubborn persistent illusion."

It would seem that 'time' requires further investigation.

First, the true nature of an 'event' needs to be considered.

An 'event' can be thought of as any everyday experience, such as going shopping, having a discussion with a friend or going out for dinner.

Whenever you decide to do something there are always different probabilities you can choose from.

Even a mundane event such as going to the shops has several probabilities.

You can either go or not go; you can use the car or walk; you can go to one particular shop in preference to another.

These are just a few of the probabilities you can choose to experience in your 'physical' reality.

However, the true nature of an 'event' is that, at some level of reality, all the probabilities exist and are part of your experience.

If this still sounds incredible, then consider the words of physicist Hugh Everett:

"Quantum physics predicts that all alternative outcomes of any given experiment must occur even though we may only see a single outcome. Somehow, those hidden alternatives must exist simultaneously along with the observed outcome."

It may help to think of an event being like an orange, which is made up of a number of segments.

Each segment is only part of the orange.

It is only when all the segments are viewed together that you consider it to be an orange.

When you experience an event in your waking state of consciousness, you are actually just experiencing one segment of the event.

You experience other segments of the event in other states of consciousness, where you use time and space in different ways.

From the point of view of your waking state of consciousness you string single segments together in normal memory to give you what you consider to be your past.

All of the segments, or probabilities, that make up a particular 'event' are determined by your personal beliefs about what is possible and what is not possible.

This is very important to remember.

It therefore follows that the difference between a probability and a possibility needs to be clarified.

In a given event there are a limited number of probabilities, but there could be an infinite number of possibilities.

As an example, in a free and democratic country it is a possibility for anyone to become Prime Minister or President.

However, it is not necessarily a probability because of other choices people have made.

To help understand these very alien concepts of the nature of an event and the simultaneous nature of time, consider the following analogy.

Imagine a large piece of material with small squares printed on it, similar to a chess board, laid out on the floor in front of you.

In this analogy each of the squares represents an event.

The squares directly in front of you represent the present time, those to your left represent the past, and those to your right represent the future.

Now imagine yourself in a 'God like' position gazing down at the squares laid out on the floor.

From this position you can see that past, present and future exist simultaneously, because you can see all the squares and therefore all the events at the same time.

Now imagine crouching down with your nose just a few inches or centimetres from the squared material on the floor.

From this position you can now only see one square, or one event.

You can not see the rest of the squares, although they still exist.

You can move your focus from one square to another depending on your choice of direction, but you only ever see 'one square at a time'.

When you move from one square to another you create an experience of time passing.

The true nature of the piece of material with squares on it does not change.

This analogy gives you an insight into how reality is experienced through the five senses 'one event at a time'.

This same analogy can be taken a little further.

Imagine returning to your 'God like' position so that you can gaze down at the sea of squares stretching out in all directions.

Now choose just one square.

This time, instead of imagining this square to be one whole event, imagine it to be one probability of an event.

Now imagine the surrounding cluster of squares touching it on each of its sides to be the other probabilities of the event.

You can now see that if you choose a different square from the cluster, that different square touches a different set of surrounding squares.

In this analogy, the different set of squares represents different probabilities that have now become available.

As stated earlier, the probabilities that are available to you in your everyday reality are determined by your beliefs.

Changing a belief is represented by choosing a different square in this analogy.

With this understanding of the true nature of an event it is possible to exercise real power.

Remember that all probabilities of an event do exist and are yours for the choosing.

This means that you can take any event in your so-called past that disturbs you and choose a more favourable outcome.

The probability that you had previously accepted as the only outcome, now takes its place in your memory as just one of a number of probable outcomes.

When you no longer attach significance to this less favourable probable outcome, it will no longer affect your 'present' experiences.

You really can choose an effectively different 'past'.

This is not self deception.

Your everyday experiences will actually change in line with this newly recognised past.

Sometimes people may question why they should have had to suffer poor experiences as a child, just because they had not yet learned about how their beliefs affect their experiences.

It can now be seen that all probabilities and all life experiences are simultaneous, therefore the beliefs of your childhood are formed not only in what you think of as your past, but also in what you think of as your present and, of course, your future.

It is only because of the piecemeal way in which you normally understand reality that you think your childhood existed before your present time.

But as the new understanding of 'time' demonstrates, it is always from the present moment that you choose your experiences, whether you call them 'past', 'present' or 'future' and these experiences are always based on your beliefs in the present moment.

It is always from the present moment that you choose what direction you will take and which probabilities you will use in your waking state of consciousness.

You do not need to believe you are a prisoner of 'karma', or fate, no matter what events you think have happened in this or any other life.

All of the probabilities of any so-called past event exist now and are just as real as the one probability remembered by 'you' in your waking state of consciousness.

Your 'present' experiences do not have to be limited by any beliefs you have about your perceived 'past', because you do not have a single fixed past.

Changing your beliefs in the present moment sets you free to choose your life experiences.

Module 3

The True Nature of Time

Test Yourself Questions

3.1   How do you comprehend time?

3.2   Describe the true nature of an event?

3.3   Describe what is meant by a 'probability' and how does it differ from a 'possibility'?

3.4   Describe briefly how to change the past.

3.5   Explain why you do not need to be a prisoner of so-called 'past life' events?

Module 4

Insights Into Reincarnation & Death

Most people will be aware of the concept of reincarnation, which will be discussed later in this module.

However, whatever you may personally think about the concept of reincarnation, it will certainly raise three other terms which need to be reassessed first.

They are the terms 'physical', 'spiritual' and 'death', which will be dealt with individually, although they are all interrelated.

The first term to consider is 'physical'.

Generally speaking, most people refer to their day to day existence as their 'physical reality'.

But what is really understood by the term 'physical reality'?

Usually, when people talk about 'physical reality' they mean tangible or solid or relating to things perceived through the five senses.

However, Module 1 demonstrated that your senses cannot be relied upon to give accurate information about the true nature of reality.

It also showed that although scientists have tried to find the smallest piece of 'physical reality', or 'solid matter', they have failed to do so.

They just end up with something called 'energy' but nobody can really explain what that is.

This indicates that there really is no such thing as a solid object in the true sense; it is just a result of perception through the five senses.

If 'solid' is how the word 'physical' is defined, then it would be equally correct to use the word 'physical' to describe objects in the dream state of consciousness, because they are 'solid' to the person who is dreaming.

To help clarify this point, try to find an alternative word to 'solid' that can describe objects in the dream state of consciousness as they 'feel' to the person who is dreaming.

It is important to realise how words in common usage can mask a true understanding.

In the context of understanding the nature of reality, it can be seen that the word 'physical' is a misleading term.

The next term to consider is 'spiritual'.

'Spiritual' is a word much used today, but probably has many different meanings to different people.

Therefore, you might like to pause and consider what the term 'spiritual' means to you.

Generally, when people speak about the 'spiritual' aspect of human beings, they are referring to an aspect that is not 'physical'.

This 'non-physical' aspect of human beings is known by many different names, dependent upon which religion or philosophy is followed.

The important point to understand is that the word 'spiritual' is meant to denote something very different and separate from the 'physical'; in particular something that is not solid or tangible, or in other words something that is 'non-physical'.

It was shown earlier that what would previously have been referred to as 'physical' is just 'a matter of perception'.

Therefore, does the term 'non-physical' really have any meaning?

It is clear that, because of the limitations of language, it is not always easy to convey the full understanding intended.

However, it has already been shown that consciousness is the ground of all being, and that matter, energy and consciousness are all the same thing.

Consequently, there can be no different and separate 'something' to which the term 'spiritual' can be attached.

It is apparent that the word 'spiritual' is also a misleading term.

There are no real differences between 'physical' and 'spiritual'; there are only different 'perceptions within consciousness'.

The final term for discussion is, appropriately, 'Death'.

This is probably the most emotive of the three terms, but with a little more understanding, it can be shown in its true perspective.

The general dictionary definition of the word 'death' is 'the destruction or end of something.'

From a personal point of view this is understood to mean the end of your life.

No matter what religion is followed, 'death' means a transition from the 'physical' to the 'spiritual'.

As already shown, the only difference between the so-called 'physical' and the so-called 'spiritual' is just a difference of perception within consciousness.

Clearly, it can be realised that all you ever do is change your perception within consciousness.

Therefore, so-called 'death' is also just a change in your perception within consciousness and, as such, is not an end of anything.

Module 3 explained the true nature of time; that all outcomes exist simultaneously; therefore it has to be true to say that the states of so-called 'life' and so-called 'death' exist simultaneously.

Consequently, you are already as dead as you ever will be.

This is quite a liberating thought, isn't it?

It is worth taking some time to consider how you think this might change your approach to life.

You may put different labels on your different perceptions within consciousness, such as 'waking state', 'dreaming state', or even 'death', but these labels are only for intellectual convenience.

There are no actual divisions in consciousness.

This statement will become clearer as you progress through the book.

It is only your beliefs about each of the labels you attach to your 'perceptions within consciousness', or 'pieces of reality', that determine your expectations and emotions concerning them.

If you misunderstand the labels you attach to those 'pieces of reality', you will have a false impression of the true nature of reality and of your own true nature.

As you learn more about your true nature, you will lose any fear you may have had about changing from one state of consciousness to another; you will see that there is no loss of continuity to your identity.

In fact, as you become more aware of your true nature, your sense of identity will grow; your sense of what is 'not you' will diminish; you will become more aware of the 'whole of reality' rather than just 'pieces of reality'.

Most people find it easy to accept that they create all objects and, of course, all concepts in the state of consciousness called 'the dream state'.

With the insights gained so far, you may now more easily accept that you create all objects and concepts in the state of consciousness called 'the waking state'.

This, of course, includes the concepts of 'physical', 'spiritual' and 'death'.

With this new understanding of these concepts, it becomes necessary to reassess the concept of reincarnation.

The traditional teaching of reincarnation is generally considered to be an Eastern religious concept, and it is certainly a major principle of both Buddhism and Hinduism.

The teaching of reincarnation states that when people die their Spirit, or Soul, survives the death of the physical body and continues in the spiritual realm.

In this spiritual realm, they review their past life and then choose another physical life, which can be either male or female and occur in any geographical location on Earth.

The new physical life that they choose will present different social and political circumstances and therefore an opportunity for different experiences.

A simple analogy would be playing different roles in different films, each role requiring a different costume and a different script.

Like any good actor who becomes totally absorbed in the role they are playing, a person becomes so absorbed in a particular 'incarnation' that they forget who and what they actually are.

However, this is necessary for the sets of circumstances which they choose to experience in their new 'incarnation' to have real meaning for them.

For instance, imagine trying to understand poverty.

So you decide to put on some old clothes and live in a cardboard box under a bridge.

Although you may be very uncomfortable for a few days living like this, you will not really understand what it is like to be poor if you know that you have a nice warm house and healthy bank account to return to.

The teachings surrounding 'reincarnation' further indicate that in choosing the circumstances for a new physical life, it is necessary to take into consideration any 'lessons of life' to be learned and atonement for any transgressions that may have been committed in any previous life.

This is, of course, where the Eastern concept of 'karma' comes into play.

The cycle of rebirth continues until all the required 'lessons of life' have been learned and any karmic debt that has accrued has been paid off.

When the cycle of rebirth is complete, which normally takes many 'lifetimes', the individual spirit will then transcend to a higher spiritual realm.

Please appreciate that this is just a brief outline of reincarnation, but it will suffice for these purposes.

The general teaching of reincarnation can now be compared with the new understanding of 'physical', 'spiritual', 'death' and the true nature of time.

The comparison highlights some contradictions.

The contradictions become apparent because the main teachings of reincarnation are based on sequential lives and the existence of two separate realms; the 'physical' and the 'spiritual'.

But, as you now know, all events exist simultaneously and the only difference between the so-called 'physical' and the so-called 'spiritual' is just a difference of perception within consciousness.

To assist with understanding this point, it may help to cast your mind back to the piece of checked material.

You may remember that from your God like position you could see so-called past, present and future existing simultaneously.

Therefore, if all time periods exist simultaneously, then the logical conclusion to be drawn from this is that all so-called reincarnations must exist simultaneously.

As all so-called reincarnations exist simultaneously, and are expressions within consciousness, 'reincarnations' can now be understood as 'probabilities set in a time frame'.

As a result of this new understanding of the concept of 'reincarnation', some people may question why they have 'felt' particularly 'connected' to 'certain characters in history'.

Remember that your personal beliefs determine the specific probabilities that you experience out of all the available probabilities.

Therefore, it is limiting your experiences to believe that you can only be 'connected' to 'certain characters in history'.

With this greater understanding, it can be seen how you can become aware of 'probabilities', which you may previously have set in a time frame and called 'reincarnations'.

This applies not only to so-called 'past' lives but also to so-called 'future' lives.

Interestingly, it is possible to find a great deal of written evidence recording what people think of as their 'past' lives, but not much about any 'future' lives.

With a little consideration on this point it can be seen that it is based on 'limiting beliefs' about time.

It is all too easy to get trapped in the belief of time starting somewhere in the past and progressing only up to the present moment.

This belief will allow the consideration of 'past' lives, but will turn a 'blind eye', so to speak, to any information considered as 'in the future', whether a 'future life' or a 'future event'.

Generally, any information about 'the future' is considered as 'clairvoyance', but this label is based on a misunderstanding about the simultaneous nature of probabilities.

There is no 'fixed' future any more than there is a fixed past.

Any future event 'seen' by a clairvoyant can now be understood as just one probability, which, dependent upon personal beliefs, may or may not be experienced in the 'waking state of consciousness'.

You now know that you exist in an ocean of consciousness, where all probabilities exist simultaneously; where you have your own individuality and at the same time are connected to and communicate with all consciousness.

Module 4

Insights Into Reincarnation & Death

Test Yourself Questions

4.1   Explain briefly the traditional understanding of reincarnation.

4.2   What do you understand by the term 'incarnation'?

4.3   Describe briefly how you would explain the simultaneous nature of time to someone.

Module 5

The Source of All 'Being'

Physical reality is not what it appears to be!

Recent estimates by NASA say that the universe is made of 73% dark energy, 23% dark matter and only 4% atomic matter.

Dark energy and dark matter are terms used by scientists to describe what they believe are fundamental phenomena of the universe but which do not comply with any known laws of physics.

This means that 96% of the universe is in a 'form' that science has no explanation for at all.

However, the situation for scientists is even more perplexing than that, because, as explained in Module 1, they really do not know what the 4% of so-called atomic matter is made of either.

This may have come as a surprise to many people because they were accustomed to scientists speaking of 'matter' as if they had already proved it was some very small and solid 'thing'.

The importance of discovering the nature of 'matter' has been clearly demonstrated by the amount of time, effort and money that has been spent on The Large Hadron Collider at Cern laboratories in Switzerland, which was switched on for its first full test in September 2008.

Similarly, although they may be accustomed to scientists speaking of the 'big bang' as the known origin of the universe, people may also be surprised to learn that this is still a theory.

In fact, there are an increasing number of scientists who now state that the current big bang theory does not hold up to scrutiny.

It is ironic that many scientists are guilty of the same error that they often level at people outside the official scientific community of not impartially examining all the evidence.

If they examined all the scientific evidence it would show that their 'materialist' view of reality is untenable.

This evidence would, of course, include the findings at the cutting edge of quantum physics that 'matter, energy and consciousness are the same thing'.

Further evidence against the 'materialist' view of reality is provided by physicist Alain Aspect and his team when, in 1982, they discovered a 'transcendent reality' beyond the normally accepted reality of spacetime.

These experiments were refined and repeated in 1997 by Dr Nicolas Gisin, the results of which confirmed the earlier findings of the Alain Aspect team.

These findings support the eastern philosophies' view that this 'transcendent reality' is 'the source of all being', which underlies the 'material reality' of spacetime that is perceived by the five senses.

This 'transcendent reality' is sometimes referred to by scientists as 'the quantum vacuum'.

Surprisingly, for most scientists, this transcendent realm, or quantum vacuum, was referred to as 'Akasha' in ancient Hindu texts, which are at least several thousand years old.

The nature of this 'transcendent realm' that is the source of all 'being' will now be explored.

However, to prevent misunderstanding it is very important that a commonly understood vocabulary is used.

You will already be familiar with the terms 'spirit' and 'soul', which are often used interchangeably in religious and philosophical discussions, but unfortunately their definitions are always vague.

Therefore these terms will not be used in this book, in order to avoid any religious or philosophical misconceptions.

When discussing 'the source of all being', the term 'Self' will be introduced in this module and used throughout the remainder of the book.

The 'Self' is not a concept that can be understood in its entirety by the intellect because 'it' cannot be defined using vocabulary or imagery.

The 'Self' perceives but cannot be perceived.

It is important that the term 'Self' is not confused with the term 'personal self', as generally referred to in traditional psychology.

However, the following statements will help provide insights into the 'nature' of the 'Self'.

The 'Self' is a state of 'being' that uses consciousness as a 'tool' to explore itself.

The 'Self' desires to know itself completely but, because of its limitless nature, is unable to do so, and herein lies the mystery of 'eternity'.

The 'Self' is the source of all states of consciousness including the 'waking state of consciousness'.

An idea of the 'Self' as 'essence' is expressed beautifully by the great sage Sri Nisargadatta Maharaj when he said,

"Existence is in consciousness, essence is independent of consciousness."

In Module 2 it was explained how your 'waking state of consciousness' is part of the 'ocean of consciousness' within which you are connected to all consciousness.

Because you have a sense of individuality you experience a 'waking state of consciousness' in your own unique and individual way.

It is important to remember that all experiences are experiences within consciousness, in whatever form they may appear.

It is also important to remember that all consciousness is connected and interacts; there are no actual divisions in consciousness.

This also means that there are no hierarchies in consciousness and therefore no divisions such as 'Human consciousness', 'Animal consciousness', 'Plant consciousness' and 'Mineral consciousness'.

There is just 'consciousness', which can 'experience' in different ways.

Understanding this very strange concept can be assisted by referring to the dream state of consciousness where all 'things' within a dream are constructions within consciousness.

Although the 'things' appear in different forms and appear separate to each other and separate to you, when you awake you realize that they are not.

They are all created from the same 'stuff' and are your own constructions within consciousness, which exist in a 'time' and 'space' framework, which is also constructed by you.

Although, from the human point of view, you are generally aware of using only one state of consciousness at a time, the 'Self' creates and uses many different states of consciousness simultaneously.

Dependent upon the literature you are familiar with, you may find some of these states of consciousness are referred to as reincarnations, probable lives, alternate lives or counterparts.

To avoid confusion, whenever you come across one of these terms, it will help to substitute it with the term 'Alternate You'.

This will help you to realize that all these different terms are just different names for what appear to be other parts of 'you' existing in what appear to be different time frames.

An analogy would be to think of these different expressions of 'you' like parts of your body.

Generally, you would not consider your hand to be less important to you than your foot.

Each of them looks different and performs different functions but is an integral part of your whole body, allowing you greater expression and experience.

There are some states of consciousness created by the 'Self' that are labelled 'ego' and 'personality'.

Within these states of consciousness, the 'Self' can explore 'its nature' using aspects of consciousness that it creates such as space, time and emotions.

It is easy to make the mistake of identifying the 'Self' as the 'personality' or 'ego', but this is not the case.

Therefore, a more detailed explanation is required as to how these particular states of consciousness operate.

It is important to remember that these explanations of 'ego' and 'personality' may differ from the traditional explanations within psychology.

To help with this more detailed explanation, consider again the large piece of material with small squares on it.

Now imagine placing a large ring randomly onto the checked material so that it encompasses a number of the small squares.

Now imagine placing a smaller ring, which only encompasses one square, on the checked material inside the larger ring.

For the purposes of this analogy, the large ring represents a state of consciousness called 'personality' and the small ring represents a state of consciousness called 'ego'.

The 'ego' equates to the 'waking state of consciousness' and is responsible for what are considered 'daily experiences'.

If you imagine that each square represents a 'probability', you can see that the larger ring, which represents the state of consciousness called 'personality', encompasses a larger number of 'probabilities' than the smaller ring.

You can see that the smaller ring, which represents the state of consciousness called 'ego', only encompasses one square or 'probability'.

If you imagine moving the small ring from square to square you can see how the 'ego' views the 'wholeness' of reality 'a piece at a time'.

This analogy also demonstrates that as the 'ego' moves from square to square it invents the concept of 'time', as it can only view one square after another.

Developing this analogy enables insights into communication with so-called 'others'.

For instance, imagine a second large ring and small ring placed similarly and adjacent to the first set of rings.

This second set of rings represents another 'personality' with an 'ego' with whom the first 'set' might communicate.

Imagine that all communication is via the 'personalities', represented by the 2 large rings, and that their 'personal realities' are experienced by the 'egos', represented by the 2 small rings.

Each 'personal reality' will be determined by the belief system held by each 'ego'.

Each belief system can be represented by the small ring surrounding the individual square.

Therefore, any communication from the 'personality' has to pass through the belief system of the 'ego'.

So, no matter how well informed the 'personality' may be, due to its larger view of reality, any communication between the 'personality' and the 'ego' can be either modified or even completely blocked by the belief system of the 'ego'.

Communication from any other 'personality' also has to pass through the belief system of each 'ego'.

This analogy demonstrates the importance of ensuring that the beliefs held by each 'ego' are as open and flexible as possible, because they directly determine the experiences by the 'ego' in each probability represented by each square.

It is important to understand that the 'Self' is aware of all the probabilities, represented by the squares both inside and outside of all the rings.

Information from the 'Self' can be conveyed to 'personality' and 'ego' at all times, but can be blocked at 'ego' level because of limiting beliefs.

However, there are certain states of consciousness where 'ego' does not operate, such as the 'dream state'.

Therefore, it is often possible for information communicated from the 'Self' to the 'personality' to be 'remembered' upon wakening.

It is important to remember that the 'ego' and 'personality' are only part of 'you'.

As explained by physics professor Amit Goswami,

"The ego is only an operational, temporary identity of the Self."

The limitations of language to describe the nature of consciousness and the realities that exist within it must always be borne in mind when contemplating the nature of the 'Self' as the source of all 'being'.

For this reason descriptions and analogies should not be taken too far in a search for an exact definition.

It is important to remember that the 'Self' is unlimited, and therefore any such definitions will always be inadequate.

You should start to think less in terms of labels and divisions in consciousness, and more in terms of consciousness operating as a 'whole'.

The concept of the 'Self' will be revisited in Module 8 after the 'apparent' nature of reality has been explained further in the next 2 modules.

Understanding the concepts introduced in this module can be assisted by contemplating the words of the sage Sri Nisargadatta Maharaj:

"Our minds are waves on the ocean of consciousness. As waves they come and go. As ocean they are infinite and eternal. Know yourself as the ocean of being."

Module 5

The Source of All 'Being'

Test Yourself Questions

5.1   What do you understand by the word 'soul'?

5.2   What do you understand by the term 'Self'?

5.3   How would you describe the meaning of the word 'consciousness' as used on the Course?

5.4   Explain what you understand by the term 'Alternate You'?

5.5   Explain the term 'ego' as used on the Course.

5.6   Explain the term 'personality' as used on the Course.

Module 6

The Nature of Illness & How to Stay Well

Have you ever thought about how you become ill?

Have you considered that your thoughts may play a role in your illness?

Would you be surprised, or even outraged, to learn that generally people put themselves in the role of 'victim' with regard to illness.

Without even realising it, most people tend to take the stance that there are various illnesses 'out there' waiting to 'get them'.

People think they can catch a disease from someone else.

But what if this is not a fact; what if this is just part of most peoples' belief system?

You may find this idea difficult to accept, because you may be wondering about all the microbes and viruses that are normally attributed to causing illness.

It may help if you consider how the concept of microbes and viruses could fit in with how you create your experiences based on what you believe is possible.

This puzzle becomes easier to understand if you remember the different people and places you create in your dream state of consciousness, and then interact with as if they are solid and separate to you.

You use the same creative process in your waking state of consciousness that you use in your dream state of consciousness.

Therefore you can see that creating a microbe or virus is no different from creating any other object.

Whatever you 'create' you interact with in accordance with your beliefs about it.

So if you believe microbes and viruses make you ill, that will be your experience.

How many times have you found yourself expecting to catch a cold because so many people are coughing and sneezing around you?

You need to change your perception of 'illness' in the same way that you changed your perception of the terms 'physical', 'spiritual' and 'death'.

Once you realize that 'illness' is a concept, and therefore subject to your beliefs about it, you can start to change your experience of it.

If you are 'ill' you should look on it in just the same way as any other experience in your life, and so examine your own thoughts and beliefs for its origin, and of course its cure.

Your natural state is 'healthy', which you can maintain perfectly well if you trust yourself to do so, and don't impede this healthy state with limiting thoughts and beliefs.

It is easy to forget that your body is your own conscious construction, just the same as any other object in your personal reality.

Your body image and health are dependent upon your total belief system, which can include concepts such as heredity, evolution, diet, disease and ageing.

You may find it useful to make a list of what you think are facts about the body as opposed to beliefs about the body.

Once you are aware that you are dealing with beliefs about the body, you can take back responsibility and stop looking to others for your well being, such as doctors, surgeons, and chemists etc.

Applying your new belief, that only you maintain your own health, should be done gradually and with care.

It will be different for each of you, dependent on your present belief system, which will include confidence in your own ability.

To build confidence, it is best to start with some small symptom of illness with which you can verify your ability to make a real change in your health.

As you gain in confidence you can progress to what you consider more difficult symptoms of illness.

The actual process of how you affect a change in health is exactly the same, whatever the type of illness.

To illustrate this point, try and think of an instance where this process would not apply.

Dependent upon your belief system, and whilst you are gaining in confidence, you may find yourself being assisted in reaching your healthy state by such people as doctors, chemists or alternative health practitioners.

This can be thought of as a 'weaning period'.

It is important to understand that whilst you still have a belief in the doctor's pills then you should continue to take them.

Sometimes you might manifest a so-called 'illness' because of a lack of understanding about a particular set of circumstances.

For instance you may believe that you are going to be faced with some unpleasant task that you can do nothing about.

As a response to this you incapacitate yourself in some way, perhaps by pulling a muscle in your back whilst digging in the garden.

This way you would give yourself the excuse not to carry out the unpleasant task.

You may be able to think of an instance in your own life where you may have created a similar scenario.

With a greater understanding of how you create your experiences you can change the 'unpleasant task' to a more pleasurable one and so avoid the need for an 'illness'.

You can now see how an illness may not be related to one isolated circumstance but to several circumstances.

These circumstances can at first appear unrelated as they may be spread out over an extended period of 'time'.

Through introspection, you can be aware of the process and the reasons involved, and make any necessary adjustments to your belief system.

Obviously everyone would wish to eliminate illness, not only from their own bodies, but also from seeing illness in other people.

It is a common misconception to think that when you 'see other people's illness' you are viewing a display of 'other people's beliefs', which have nothing to do with your own personal belief system.

However, what you see in 'others' is actually a reflection of your own belief system.

In the context of what you have learned so far, try and think of a circumstance where you do not think you are viewing your own beliefs in action.

You may recall from Module 5 that in the state of consciousness called 'ego', you create your 'personal' experiences.

Therefore, under normal circumstances, it is impossible to see someone else's 'personal' experiences, just as whilst dreaming it is impossible to see someone else's 'personal' dream.

Remember that communications concerning spacetime and emotions are filtered through created states of consciousness that are called 'personality' and 'ego'.

The communications that pass through the 'ego's' belief system become your 'waking state' reality.

Therefore you can now see that everything in your personal reality is based solely on your belief system, which includes seeing illness in other people.

For some people this may create a dilemma.

For instance, if you are in a healing profession of any kind, whether you are a doctor, surgeon or alternative practitioner, you have a belief in illness.

You expect to see illness in other people; in fact your job depends on it.

The situation may occur that you wish to change your beliefs in order to eliminate illness from your experience, but by doing so, it may remove the need for your job.

In some instances, what is required is a new way of looking at your chosen career.

As an example, if you were an aromatherapist who normally expected to have people coming to you with various illnesses to be treated, you could now expect healthy people to come to you because they wanted to experience the undoubted relaxation of an aromatherapy massage.

In this example your beliefs are now in harmony with your preferred experiences.

If, on the other hand, you happened to be a heart transplant surgeon but wanted to eliminate illness from your experience it would of course be impossible to expect healthy people to come to you for heart transplants.

To illustrate the point, it may be helpful to consider other occupations where people may have a similar dilemma.

There are no rights or wrongs to any career; it is all about personal choice as to what experiences you want in your life.

Because you create your own personal experiences based on your beliefs about what is possible, you will be able to change your expectations about illness in yourself and others.

You will therefore be able to banish illness from your day to day experience.

This is quite a concept to take in, isn't it?

Logically of course it would have to be this way, bearing in mind what you have learned so far.

Module 6

The Nature of Illness & How to Stay Well

Test Yourself Questions

6.1   How do you get ill as explained on the Course?

6.2   How do you stay well as explained on the Course?

6.3   How does the Course explain such things as microbes and viruses and their role in illness?

6.4   How does the concept of 'creating your own experiences' impact on the healing professions?

Module 7

The True Nature of Dreams

The dream state of consciousness is an important reference for understanding altered states of consciousness.

A more detailed exploration will also provide further insights into reality itself.

You may find it useful to consider your own thoughts about the state of consciousness called 'dreaming'?

It is fair to say that 'dreaming' is a different state of consciousness, with a reality just as 'real' and valid as the waking state, but without the same strict confines of time and space.

Because of this, 'action' may not be perceived as a series of moments one following the other.

Even though you may accept the last statement, it may still come as a surprise to learn that the 'dream state' does not begin or end.

Your dream state of consciousness exists constantly alongside your waking state of consciousness.

This statement becomes easier to comprehend the more you think of your day to day reality as a state of consciousness.

You also need to stop thinking of the dream state of consciousness as something unreal or imaginary.

It is only if 'personality' becomes too intensely focused through its 'ego' state of consciousness that it becomes unaware of other states of consciousness such as the dream state.

To help you understand how you alter your focus between these two states of consciousness called 'waking state' and 'dream state', consider the following analogy.

Imagine you have 2 televisions back to back and each of them is tuned to a different television station.

Imagine one television to represent the 'waking state' and the other television to represent the 'dream state'.

In this analogy, 'you' represent the state of consciousness called 'personality'.

If you were to walk from one television to the other, you would be able to alternate between what was happening in the 'waking state' and what was happening in the 'dream state' but would not be able to see both at the same time.

This analogy represents 2 states of consciousness operating simultaneously but you only focus on one state of consciousness at a time.

To take this analogy a little further, imagine that you now turn both televisions to face you.

You can now see both states of consciousness at the same time.

This movement of the televisions represents a change in your state of consciousness to one of expanded awareness.

This new state of consciousness can continue to expand and thereby take in still more states of consciousness simultaneously.

These concepts become easier to understand as you realise that you are a conscious 'being' who changes states of consciousness.

Generally people tend to be more familiar with two of these states of consciousness, the waking state of consciousness and the dreaming state of consciousness, but these are just names.

It is unfortunate that the word 'dream' is associated with the word 'unreal', because this way of thinking sets up barriers to understanding states of consciousness.

However, there is another state of consciousness that you are familiar with.

It is easy to overlook the fact that 'imagination' is a state of consciousness.

The state of consciousness called 'imagination' can be considered a 'stepping stone' between the waking state of consciousness and the dreaming state of consciousness.

Now return to the analogy of the 2 televisions side by side and facing you with each television tuned to a different channel.

However this time, one television will represent the 'waking' state and the other will represent the state of 'imagination'.

If you sit in front of the televisions but concentrate on the one called 'imagination', you will now only vaguely be aware of what is happening on the other television called 'waking' state.

Like the dream state of consciousness, 'imagination' is free of many of the restrictions of time and space that apply to the waking state of consciousness.

People may not appreciate the creative potential of the state of consciousness called 'imagination', because it is often considered 'make-believe' and of no real importance.

With greater understanding about different states of consciousness, you can put this knowledge to more creative use.

For instance, you can use imagination and your understanding about probabilities to create the most desirable probable past and the most desirable probable future.

Working with imagination in this way becomes easier when you realise that your so-called past and future are just probabilities in a time setting.

You have different opportunities for creativity in the dream state of consciousness, where you do not have the same restrictions of time and space that you have in the 'waking' state of consciousness.

In the dream state you use time and space very differently, even to the extent of not using time and space at all, but of course this is not possible to talk about because of the limitations of intellect and language.

Therefore in the dream state you can explore actions and situations with far greater freedom.

Despite this greater freedom you may not choose the dream state as the most suitable for exploring a particular situation.

You may therefore decide to explore the chosen situation within the normal confines of time and space in your waking state.

Whilst exploring a particular situation, and in order to overcome a particular limiting belief, you may use illness or some uncomfortable psychological condition to help you further your understanding.

Whilst exploring situations in the dream state of consciousness, you may find yourself involved in activities that seem surprising or even out of character.

These situations are examples of other probabilities that you are exploring.

In the dream state you can experience any probability, which includes those in different time frames that you would normally think of as past, present and future.

This is possible because the usual barriers of how you experience time do not exist in that state of consciousness.

It is worth pondering at this point what you understand by the term 'Sleep'?

When you think about it carefully you will see that 'sleep' is, in fact, an altered state of consciousness.

In your waking state of consciousness you sometimes remember images and experiences from the state of consciousness called 'sleep'.

It is these images and experiences that are then referred to as your dreams.

When you are in the state of consciousness called 'sleep', the 'personality' is not focused in the 'waking state' of consciousness.

In this less restricted state of consciousness you may more easily allow through communications from other states of consciousness.

These communications may result in a 'dream', which will provide you with more information about the true nature of reality and so allow you to make better value judgements.

From the point of view of the 'Self' there is no real distinction made between 'exterior' or 'interior' actions, it is only in your waking state of consciousness that you make those distinctions.

That is why 'sorting out a problem' in the altered state of consciousness called dream, is just as effective as sorting it out in the waking state of consciousness known as everyday reality.

The dream state of consciousness should be seen as an inexhaustible source of information.

However, you may use personalised symbolism to communicate ideas and information between your various states of consciousness.

For instance, you may represent overcoming difficulties with the symbolism of climbing mountains or other structures.

Therefore it can be quite useful to try and understand the personalised symbolism you use in your dream state of consciousness.

It is worth remembering that there is no fixed 'system' of symbolism; therefore you have to intuitively recognise for yourself what your personalised symbolism means.

Alternatively, you may not use personalised symbolism, in which case being aware of the general impression of a dream is just as beneficial.

If you wish, as an exercise, before you go to sleep each night, tell yourself that you are going to remember your dreams.

You can then go on to suggest that you become more aware in that state of consciousness.

You will eventually be able to periodically direct the course of your dream life and more actively use that state of consciousness to solve problems.

However, don't worry if you are not having much success in this field.

Your dream state of consciousness will always be beneficial to you, even if you are not aware of your dreams.

Module 7

The True Nature of Dreams

Test Yourself Questions

7.1   Explain what a dream is.

7.2   Name three states of consciousness that you are familiar with.

7.3   What is the most common use for the state of 'imagination'?

7.4   Explain briefly how you can use the dream state of consciousness to advantage.

Module 8

The True Nature of World Events

So far, the main considerations have been the consequences of your beliefs on your individual life, but there is a bigger picture to consider.

As you create your own personal experiences, you need to consider what you are dealing with in relation to a world event such as an earthquake disaster or a war which may involve thousands of people.

In order for you to consider this point fully, you need to remember how you experience 'reality'.

Whatever you may previously have thought about the nature of reality, there is a perception of reality which is common to everyone.

Simply put, everyone categorises their experiences as either what goes on in 'their head' or what goes on 'external' to them.

However, even medical science says that awareness of the so-called external world can only occur inside the head, because the optical and auditory images are formed inside the brain.

Someone once said

"No one ever saw a picture in an art gallery. You always see the picture in your head."

It could be said therefore that you only have 'internal' experiences.

Remember, in a 'dream' you are having an 'internal' experience that you interact with as if it is solid, separate and external to you.

In your waking state of consciousness you interact with these internal experiences in just the same way as you interact with your 'dream' internal experiences.

In both your 'waking state' and 'dream state' you have the common experience of your 'conscious self' being separate from the world you are experiencing.

This common everyday experience is referred to as 'dualism'.

The concept of 'dualism' states that consciousness and body exist in two different realms, 'physical' and 'non-physical'.

Modern physics shows that this concept violates the laws of conservation of energy and momentum.

In order to obey these laws any interactions between different realms would result in a change of energy and momentum.

However, science always finds the energy and momentum of objects in the 'physical' world to remain exactly the same.

Because the laws of conservation of energy and momentum are well established, consciousness and what is thought of as 'physical' must exist in the same realm.

Physics knows that consciousness exhibits a quality that the so-called 'physical world' does not exhibit, that quality is known by physicists as 'nonlocality'.

The term 'nonlocality' basically means an instantaneous influence or communication without any exchange of signals through space-time, as demonstrated by such phenomena as telepathy and remote viewing.

This would place consciousness as primary to the so-called 'physical', which would mean that consciousness is the underlying reality out of which the so-called 'physical' arises.

As all so-called 'physical' things arise out of consciousness, this would have to include what is normally thought of as space and time.

These concepts are summarised by the statement from the physicist John Wheeler when he said:

"Useful as it is under everyday circumstances to say that the world exists 'out there' independent of us, that view can no longer be upheld."

If there is not "a world existing 'out there' independent of us", what is the 'reality' of a world event such as a volcanic eruption involving thousands of people?

As you think about this question, you can see that one of the most difficult aspects to understand is that of the 'other people' involved.

When 'viewing' the actions of 'other people' it is very easy to fall into the trap of thinking you are seeing someone else's reality that is separate and independent of you.

This of course cannot be true; otherwise everything that has been explained so far, which is supported by the disciplines of philosophy and physics, would be wrong.

What is needed is a completely new way of looking at 'everyday reality'.

Generally, the mistake that is often made is trying to understand reality by examining the 'bits and pieces'.

This makes it almost impossible to see what the bigger picture is; in just the same way as examining the bits and pieces of a jigsaw puzzle makes it almost impossible to understand what the entire jigsaw picture looks like.

So, to help understand reality better, what is needed is a 'top down' view rather than the 'bottom up' view that is usually taken.

So far, the 'bottom up' view has been used on this Course in order for the intellect to understand the apparent nature of reality a little better.

The intellect is now in a position to take a 'top down' view, which needs to be from the position of the Self, or at least as near as possible from an intellectual point of view.

From the position of the Self, which is the true nature of 'being', everything is 'one'; there is no separation or objectification.

The position of the Self is a point of 'knowing all', but to 'experience all' requires the creation of spacetime.

It would be rather like just reading books to learn everything there is to know about swimming.

It is only when you get into the water and actually swim that you can have the complete understanding of 'swimming'.

The Self is not a personalised term, there is not a collection of 'Selves', the Self is unity, it is the 'One' of which many eastern religions speak.

It is the source of the 'God' concept of the western religions.

It is 'All That Is'.

The Self desires to know itself completely but because of its limitless nature it is unable to do so.

In the words of Professor Amit Goswami:

"We choose our conscious experiences, yet remain 'unconscious' of the underlying process. It is this 'unconsciousness' that leads to the illusory separateness, the identity with the separate 'I' of self-reference, rather than the 'we' of unitive consciousness."

From the position of the Self, concepts are explored using consciousness, which is the medium of expression of the Self but contained within the Self.

This is beautifully expressed in the words of the great Eastern mystic, Bhagavan Sri Ramana Maharshi when he said:

"The knower is ever greater than the known, and the seer is greater than the seen. That which is known is contained within the knower, and that which is seen is in the seer; the vast expanse of the sky is in the mind, not outside, because the mind is everywhere and there is no outside to it."

The very act of exploration requires the 'one' to appear as the 'many'.

It gives birth to such concepts as 'personalisation' and 'separation'.

These concepts are expressed in vocabulary by such terms as 'I', 'you', 'we', and 'them'.

From the top down view of the Self, it is understood that these are just concepts for the purpose of exploration; therefore the Self is not lost in personal identification and separation.

But from the bottom up view, the mistake can be made of totally identifying with these concepts of 'I' and 'you' and this can give rise to feelings of separation and isolation.

As physicist Professor Amit Goswami said;

"The existence in language of such terms as 'I' and 'my', leads us into a dualistic trap. We think of ourselves as separate because we speak of ourselves in that way."

It is perhaps easier to understand this process by considering what happens in the dream state of consciousness.

You create and interact with all kinds of images and scenarios, which can sometimes produce quite emotional reactions.

You could for example create a scenario in your dream state of an earthquake that results in many people dying and as a result you can become very emotional at the 'sight' of such a tragedy because you personally identify with the imagery.

You do this because during the 'dream' you are not aware that it is 'you' who has created the imagery.

However on waking you then realise that it was 'just a dream', and are then happy that 'it did not really happen' and lots of people did not really die, but when you were in the dream it certainly felt completely 'real'.

You can also create such an image in your imagination whereby an earthquake occurs but because you view it from 'just your imagination'; you regard it as 'unreal', that people have not really just died, and therefore your emotions are not engaged in quite the same way.

In a similar way, the Self completely understands that consciousness cannot be destroyed and also knows the true nature of the imagery.

Therefore, all explorations using consciousness are 'viewed' from a point of understanding that is not swamped by emotional energy.

It is important to realise that getting carried away by emotions keeps you locked in misunderstanding the true nature of the imagery.

However, this is not to deny the importance and relevance of having emotions; they are part of the creative energy used in exploring concepts.

You can now see how similar your waking state of consciousness is to your dream state of consciousness, because whilst you are so intently focused in either of these states of consciousness you forget that you are creating the imagery and therefore you personally and emotionally identify with it as if it is solid and separate to you.

The imagery is all the more compelling when it is personalised in the form of mother, father, brother, sister and indeed your own personal body-image.

Even the concepts of 'personality' and 'ego' are limitations on what you really are, because there are no actual divisions in consciousness.

Again, it is important to understand that the true existence of all things is in the mystery of the Self, not in the imagery of spacetime.

It is perhaps easier to comprehend this if you think of your true existence and communications as being in the Self, and if you want to explore certain concepts you personalise and objectify them in states of consciousness that are called the 'waking state' and 'dream state'.

This is what the mystics of the East have tried to explain when they have referred to everyday reality as the world of illusion.

This is the concept that physicists are struggling to explain when they state that they no longer consider the world as being 'out there' separate to you, which of course includes all that is thought of as the individual people you interact with.

So, whatever you experience in your waking state of consciousness will be based on your perceived limitations, and this will include what you think of as good and evil.

As already shown, space and time are concepts, not absolutes; in the same way, good and evil are also concepts, not absolutes.

They are concepts based on value judgements made by only taking the limited 'bottom up' view of reality.

No matter how repulsive an action is that you see being committed, it will be based on your beliefs about what is possible, not of course on what you find desirable.

It is very important to remember the distinction between what you desire and what you actually believe is possible.

This is not condoning bad behaviour or suggesting that you should 'turn the other cheek'; it is stating that you create your own experiences in all their aspects.

All aspects of your experience are based on your perceived limitations about what is possible and therefore can be changed for a more favourable experience.

Once again, this is beautifully put in the words of another of the East's great modern mystics; Sri Nisargadatta Maharaj:

"You have made this world and you can change it. The world, of which you are the only source and ground, is fully within your power to change. What is created can always be dissolved and re-created. All will happen as you want it, provided you really want it. You have created the world's sorrows out of your own desires and fears, you deal with them. All is due to your having forgotten your own being. Having given reality to the picture on the screen, you love its people and suffer for them and seek to save them. It is just not so. You must begin with yourself. There is no other way."

Module 8

The True Nature of World Events

Test Yourself Questions

8.1   Explain what is happening when you view an event such as a war and also an event such as a quarrel with a neighbour?

8.2   How does the 'ego' interact with other 'personalities' in a so-called world event?

8.3   What is the most common mistake people make that causes them to misjudge what is happening in a world event?

8.4   How would you explain if 'evil' truly exists or not?

Module 9

The Magical Approach to Living

The 'magical' approach to living is both simple and natural, but it does require a radically new way of thinking.

You may have become accustomed to thinking of yourself as just flesh and blood; that you just have logic and intellect to sort your way through the challenges of life.

Nothing could be further from the truth.

These are very exciting times because science is now approaching an understanding of many of the concepts put forward in the ancient wisdom philosophies.

Quantum physics in particular is at the forefront of the sciences in discovering this radically new way of explaining reality.

There are an increasing number of quantum physicists who are at last presenting these new findings to the public without fear of ridicule from their fellow scientists.

Ideas such as 'an object is not independent of the observer; past, present and future exist simultaneously; the existence of multiple universes; and a unifying energy that underlies all realities' are discussed openly at the highest levels of physics.

Physicist Professor Amit Goswami has stated quite clearly that matter, energy and consciousness are the same thing.

This concept alone completely revolutionises the old ways of understanding the nature of reality and 'humanity's' role within it.

It opens the way for established science to also recognise a new way of living.

It is this new seemingly magical approach to living that will now be discussed.

The 'magical' approach requires a radically new approach to dealing with problems, achieving goals and in fact everything in life.

Life should be thought of as a journey of discovery, in particular a discovery of 'Self' and your true potential.

This journey has often been described in the myths and legends of ancient times as the journey of heroes.

But it is really the personal journey of Self discovery and is no less heroic.

The experiences of the journey will be unique to each person, but the goal will always be the same; to Know Your Self.

Unlike the heroic journeys of myths and legends, your journey does not have to be filled with dragons and hardships.

In fact it can be just the reverse; your journey can be inspiring and joyful.

You may create certain challenges along the way, but you should recognise them as opportunities to learn more about your true nature and your ability to create your own personal experiences.

After all, you are the creator as well as the hero of your own unique journey!

You can now recognise that these challenges represent your fears and worries which are created by limiting beliefs about yourself and what you think is possible and what is not.

Your new understanding of the nature of reality now allows you to change those beliefs and become what you are capable of becoming.

You can now truly start to realise the full potential of your creativity.

However, you should not expect that the full 'magic' of your creativity can be contained within 'clock time', nor should you think that intellect alone contains the full extent of your creativity.

You may sometimes find that the challenge with which you have confronted yourself does not seem to make much sense, from a logical point of view.

This is because the intellect, which uses time and space to view reality, attempts to break the wholeness of reality into small bits and pieces much like the pieces of a jigsaw puzzle.

Just as you would have great difficulty in guessing what the whole picture is meant to be just by looking at one piece of the jigsaw, so the intellect can make wrong assumptions about a situation because it only sees one portion of reality at a time.

You may be so used to thinking that only logic or intellect can solve your problem that you fall into the trap of forgetting you have at your disposal that other powerful tool called intuition, which can see a much larger portion of reality and so can make better judgements.

As you learn to recognise that the intellect cannot deal with everything by itself, nor does it need to, you will more easily let the intellect do what it does best, which is to deal with time and space.

Just because you may not be 'physically' doing something about a certain challenge within your waking state of consciousness, it does not mean that you are not dealing with it using other areas of your 'being'.

Therefore, on those occasions when logic cannot make sense of a particular situation, you must implement the natural way of working; which is to let go of 'the logical approach' and engage 'the magical approach'.

The more you understand this, the more comfortable you will feel about intellect working in cooperation with intuition, expecting the best outcome and not worrying about trying to understand the details.

This is a truly 'magical approach' of integrating your whole 'being' rather than just trying to use a part of it.

Another important and liberating aspect of the magical approach to living is the concept of living in the present moment.

This is utilising the concept of past, present and future existing simultaneously.

You now know that you do not have a fixed past or future and that all your experiences stem from the beliefs you hold in the present moment, which in truth is all there is.

It therefore follows from this that all your attention should be focused on living and creating in the present moment.

You should not be distracted by what you think of as a fixed past, because this does not exist any more than a fixed future exists.

Believing in a fixed past would be like carrying with you the stepping stones you have just walked over in order to cross the river.

Believing in a fixed future would be like an artist believing there is only one picture they could paint.

The only 'rule' that you should remember, whilst creating the experiences you want, is to 'create with good intent'.

As you realise that the only limitations you face are your limiting beliefs, then by acting with good intent in all your actions, you can overcome those limitations.

Acting with good intent can perhaps be best thought of as ensuring that whatever you do is not intended to cause harm.

This does not mean you have to devote yourself to a life of self sacrifice or put up with bad behaviour, as it is important that you act with good intent towards yourself as well as to others.

As part of understanding who you are, it is important that you fully understand who 'other people' are within your personal reality.

It is a common misunderstanding to think that because you create all aspects of your experiences, then all the people you meet are just figments of your imagination; that you are basically just talking to yourself and therefore relationships are meaningless.

This is definitely not the case.

It may seem this way if you insist on trying to understand the nature of reality only from the 'bottom up' point of view of the intellect, because the intellect deals in terms of 'personalisation, separation and objectification'.

Your true nature is in the 'oneness' of the 'Self', but any sense of 'oneness' is an alien concept to intellect because it implies loss of identity.

Intellect alone cannot understand how you can be 'one' and experience individuality at the same time.

In order to explore its nature, states of consciousness are created by 'the one' appearing as 'the many'.

These states of consciousness are experienced 'as if individually' using what appears to be personalised and individualised sets of beliefs.

Just as you create all the 'other people' in your dream, you also create your own body-image in your dream.

You then interact with the 'other people' as if they are 'real' and solid and separate from you.

Whilst you are 'dreaming' everything appears 'real' and you are not aware that you are the creator of all the objects and all the 'other people' in your dream.

The state of consciousness called 'waking reality' is just the same; you create all the objects and all the 'other people', including your own body image, in just the same way.

Whilst you are personalising and objectifying your creations you are unaware of yourself as the 'one consciousness' that is the creator of all realities.

Again, words are inadequate to fully explain this relationship as they trap you into speaking in terms of 'I', 'we', 'you', which give the false impression of separateness.

This inadequacy of words may give the impression, when dealing with 'other people', that you are just talking to 'yourself' or having a relationship with 'yourself'.

This is because intellect can only take the 'bottom up' view of personalisation and separation and therefore cannot understand your true nature of being 'one' but appearing as 'many'.

In order for the 'one consciousness', that you truly are, to explore itself, it appears as all the objects, people, animals and plants that you experience in your 'daily reality'.

As the 'one consciousness' you do this in order to create scenarios for interaction and learning in just the same way that you do in a so-called dream.

Therefore all interactions and relationships are important, whether they seem to be between people, animals, plants or minerals. There are no hierarchies in consciousness, there are just different forms.

This is what the ancient wisdom philosophies were alluding to when they stated that you should love all, that you should treat everyone and everything as 'yourself', because in truth everything is 'yourself'.

Even when you are operating in your 'bottom up' mode of dealing with reality, you are, in truth, constantly connected with everything in all realities, so how can you possibly ever be alone?

You are connected to all consciousness, in whatever form you may perceive it.

As you learn to view reality from the 'top down', the apparent divisions between what you consider 'you' and 'not you' will dissolve.

This allows you to draw strength and inspiration from your truly limitless nature.

As you become more aware of your true nature of 'oneness', you will find it easier to perform the juggling act of seeming like a separate individual, when you take the 'bottom up' view, but actually knowing that you are not a separate individual; that you are 'one' with all, when you take the 'top down' view.

This knowledge will allow you to understand how not to accept 'bad behaviour', but also not to fall into the trap of believing that there is a solid, separate person 'out there' outside of your control who is intent on causing you harm.

Your true nature is the 'Self', which is timeless and immortal.

The realities you experience are states of consciousness constructed from the beliefs you hold about what is possible and what is not.

This is true about each of the realities you inhabit no matter how you manipulate time and space, or if indeed you use time and space at all.

This reality should not be thought of as 'inferior' in some way to other realities.

It should be understood that you operate in all realities simultaneously and they are all interdependent.

It is not the case that you have to progress from this reality to another in some hierarchical system.

You are the great mystery of 'All That Is', where you are 'One' and individual at the same time.

This mystery cannot be comprehended by intellect alone, which can only deal with the wholeness of reality in a piecemeal fashion.

This state of 'Oneness' is beyond time and space and therefore cannot be described in the words of intellect; it requires your intuition which 'knows it' by 'being it'.

Module 9

The Magical Approach to Living

Test Yourself Questions

9.1   Give a couple of examples of how the Course has altered your approach to life.

9.2   Give an example of the difference between desire and expectation.

9.3   What aspect of the Course do you find the most challenging?

9.4   Explain how you view a relationship between yourself and another person.

9.5   When confronted by a problem, what is a quick way to regain perspective?

Epilogue

You have been shown a very different way to view reality and your part in it.

This new information has probably turned upside down your original understanding of how things are.

Incredible as this new information may seem, it is nonetheless true.

You have been given a toolbox to assist you with creating the experiences you want.

But like all toolboxes, unless you open it and use the tools, you will not achieve anything.

When confronted by any problem, a quick way to regain perspective is to ask yourself the question,

"Who is in charge of my experiences and what do I want?"

The answer of course, in case you were in any doubt, is that you are in charge and you can have anything you want, but always remember to create with good intent!

Know Your Self and enjoy your creations.

NoR

25571833R00060

Made in the USA
Charleston, SC
04 January 2014